Voice of Nature
Listen Think Act

A collection of poems on Nature and Environment.

A call to cherish the beauty of Mother Nature, listen to
her voice, think of it

Tribikram Nayak

BookLeaf
Publishing

India | USA | UK

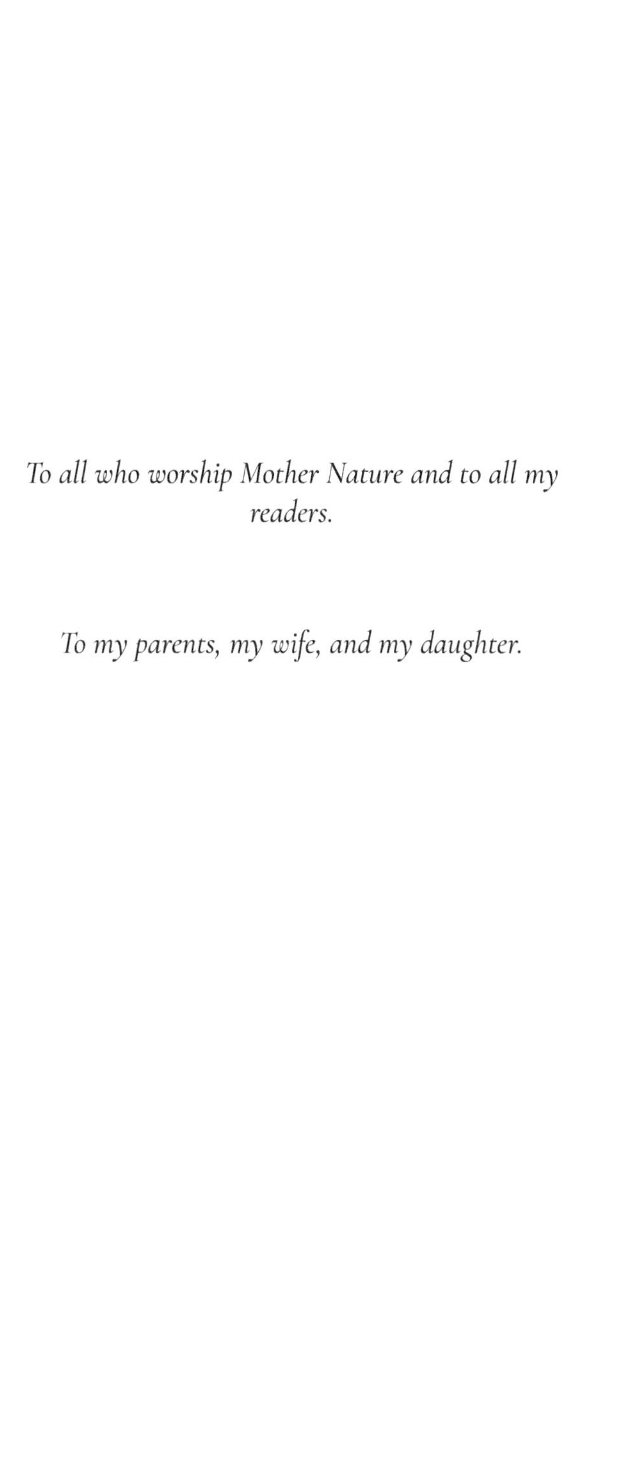

To all who worship Mother Nature and to all my readers.

To my parents, my wife, and my daughter.

Acknowledgement

In acknowledging the support of individuals and institutions, I would like to take responsibility for the views and descriptions shared in this book.

First, I would like to thank God for bestowing me with the creativity and belief to write this book.

To my wife, Sujata, for encouraging me to write and transfer my writings from the notebook to a real book.

To my daughter, Shuchiprabha, for her trust in my ability and inventiveness. Her discussion of my poems always brings new insights to the topic.

To the intellectual world of nature lovers, environmentalists and activists for their research and writings that are a constant source of inspiration for me.

To the entire team of BookLeaf Publishing for their unwavering support in converting a raw manuscript into a wonderful book. Without their efforts, I would not have become a published author.

Finally, thank you to anyone who has supported this book in any way.

Preface

The book *Voice of Nature - Listen Think Act* is a collection of poems on Nature and Environment. A call to cherish the beauty of Mother Nature, listen to her voice, think of it, and take action to protect her.

This book contains my soulful tributes to the beauty of Mother Nature. From the night sky she so beautifully decorated, to the birds she adorns with sweet voices, Nature inspires endless praise. The scenes of a forest, and the wonderful colors of the sky in the morning and in the evening steal our hearts. I can continue talking about the exquisiteness of Nature.

My heartfelt gratitude for what she provides us in every step of our lives. She gives food to our bodies and nourishes our eyes. She offers emotions and spirituality for our souls. She arranges for everything we need to survive and live a life full of LIVING.

My sincere concerns over harmful actions that we, as human beings, inflict upon

Mother Nature. We put the patience of Mother Nature to Test. We take many actions without thinking about sustainability. Mother Nature is hurt by our greediness. In this book, I call for change—actions of doing more good than harm to the environment.

We can see the impacts of neglecting our responsibility towards Nature. Extreme heat waves, frequent cyclones, severe floods and droughts, frightening sea level rise, etc. have already started to trouble us. Let's listen to the voice of Mother Nature. Let's think about what we are doing, what we are getting for us and what we are passing on to our future generations. Let's act. Even a small step of doing good for the environment will return to us with interest. Let's make a united effort. One small action in a large quantity will make the difference. Time is slipping from our hands. Let's save Mother Nature! Let's save ourselves! Let's save our future generation!

Amazing Morning

At dawn one Monday in the balcony, I stood
facing the East
Stretching hands and legs
Eyes closed for eight hours long
Yawning, trying to wake up
Amid the powerful sound of a conch shell
from the nearby priest.

Slowly tearing out the eastern sky, raised his
head the morning sun
Blooming like a red lily flower
Floating freely in a red ocean
Painting water in a color of its own
Conveyed messages with an innocent smile,
"The day has begun".

Came to me with morning rays, gifting noble
love unspoken
Red, energetic rays of the sun
entered into both my eyes
Sipped through nerves to the brain
An irrefutable command came in response,
made two eyes wide open.

Scenic beauty with all purity and caress
poured on me
No waiting, it trickled down
Heart enlightened, mind on
New energy, untold joy
Positive thoughts inside the body, like sparks
buzzing like a bee.

A gust of cool wind passed that time by,
touching my face
Spirited me double
Provided newness
Made ready for the entire day
Giving confidence to move and win through
its warm embrace.

Nature's treasure is open for us with no
guards at its doors
To enjoy as much as we can
With a smile on face, always it gives
Never-ending happiness to all
From young to old and rich to poor, all
drawing from its megastores.

Inhumane Gratitude

NATURE provides us with life!
Nutrient-rich Soil
Microbes' home Soil
On it we plough, and food we grow,
Necessary body-energy
Strength to survive
We get from the food that makes our faces
glow.

A network of rivers
Beautiful streams
Exploiting as required, we get water to live,
Needed minerals
with bountiful presence

Acting as the driver of our life-vehicle to drive.

NATURE's Atmosphere
Most essential oxygen
With no restrictions, for us to inhale it open,
Nurtures lungs
Heart, brain, and cells
Serves even the body's smallest parts with its touch golden.

NATURE's energy source
The sun's heat and light
makes all lives possible on Earth,
Needs or wants
Always ready
To fulfil our wishes to death from birth.

Numerous trees
Beautiful flowers
Blue sky and gorgeous rainbow,
Nectar from beehives
Peaceful spring wind
Green carpets and white sheets of snow.

NATURE's generosity
Giving with an open heart
Everything always to live we need,
Not considering
Even a bit of
its motherly nature and fatherly deed.

Never-ending hunger
of wealth and profit
Selfish blindness, no care for Nature, with a
hara-kiri attitude,
Non-functional conscious minds
Shallow actions of protection
Shown through deeds of humans,
an inhumane gratitude.

When will you wake up?

Took the Bay of Bengal as the origin
Wind and rain were invited in
Money and muscles faded away
Scientific power was put at bay
How can your eyes still be covered up!
When will you wake up?

Wild wind and the terrible rain
Swept habitats with no bargain
Enormous trees and tight roofs
Uprooted by squall's harsh hoofs
How can your eyes still be covered up!
When will you wake up?

May be the sound of devastation
Blocking victims' plight narration
Loud moans couldn't hit your ears
As you are in hibernation like a bear
How can your ears still be plugged up!
When will you wake up?

Maybe the rain's non-stop flow
Washed the tears, you couldn't know
People died and families cried
Attacked with vigor mercy denied
How can your eyes still be covered up!
When will you wake up?

This is the story of one 'Amphan'
Many such before have come and gone
Lots are in the factory of NATURE's anger
Under production with warning clangor
How can your eyes still be covered up!
When will you wake up?

Wake up, man, wake your conscience up!
From your head, clean dust of pretension up
Dissolve ego of money and scientific power
Work, so Nature pours its blissful shower

Build a strong relation again with Nature
Take care of plants and other creatures
Wake up, man, wake your conscience up!
From your head, clean dust of pretension up!

To save physical elements, act! Do not rest
Oceans, air, land, already stressed, satisfying
your greedy quest
No power can save you from NATURE's fury
Only humble submission for the task will
grant pardon from its jury
Before the butter melts off the bread, wake
up!
Wake up, man, wake your conscience up!
From your head, clean dust of pretension up!

Peepal I am!

Teacher entered with a book and a pen
"Here is an exciting puzzle to solve, oh!
Children."

Thirty meters high standing tall in most
villages I stay
Tired farmers or children under me I allowed
to sleep and play
Heart-shaped with long tips, my leaves
respect even the tiny wind
Start dancing with a rustling sound to give
peace to your mind
Find out children and tell who I am!
So, children, now I say, PEEPAL I AM!

Teacher entered with a book and a pen
"Here is an exciting puzzle to solve, oh!
Children."
Ficus Religiosa, some people gave me the
name
Hindus, Buddhists, and Jains keep me at the
height of my fame
Three hundred centimeters long rope can
circle my trunk
Enlightenment brought to self, sitting under
me Buddha, the great monk
Find out children and tell who I am!
So, children, now I say, PEEPAL I AM!

Teacher entered with a book and a pen
"Here is an exciting puzzle to solve, oh!
Children."
Long productive life I have, hundreds of years
to serve you
'Jay Sri Maha Bodhi' is two thousand years
old! Doesn't it amaze you?
Shelter for birds and shades for you selflessly
I provide

Fodder for animals, and fertility to soil I give
with pride
Find out children and tell who I am!
So, children, now I say, PEEPAL I AM!

Teacher entered with a book and a pen
"Here is an exciting puzzle to solve, oh!
Children."
My bark, leaves, fruits, roots, and seeds are for
everybody
To utilize in medicines, for healing ailments
of human body
Highest amount of oxygen I release, people
say
My leaves can show the presence of pollutants
in air always
Find out children and tell who I am!
Children shouted loud and clear, PEEPAL I
AM!

Breathing is not Free

A letter dropped at my door,
Hearing something fall, outside I came.
Saw a packet mat finished lotus-colored,
Bound in a braided golden thread of silk.
Looked around, found nobody.
Hesitating in my heart, I picked the packet
up.
In green glitter pen on it written was my
name,
A letter dropped at my door,
Hearing something fall, outside I came.

Opening the cover I saw,
Two sheets of handmade paper, jasmine
flowers painted on.
Written in red,
The letter in my name from future, a message
to mourn,
Opening the cover I saw,
Two sheets of handmade paper, jasmine
flowers painted on.

Standing there with eyes wide open,
Impatiently started reading line-by-line, no
blinking.
The first sheet stated,
"Nature offered air for no cost,
Oxygen loaded, and
Other elements needed
Refilling always, never exhaustive.

Warned humans to maintain balance,
Industries started,
Money flooded,
The demon of greed came in sequence.

The Man ignored the priceless gift,
Egoism spread,
Cataract occurred,
'I and Me' attitude blocked his vision to see
the unsafe shift.

Poisonous wastes dumped in the basket of
Nature,
Air became sick,
Refueling the system broken,
Forest destroyed, leaving Earth's lungs to
rupture.
Men's deeds upset system of natural
purification,
Uncontrolled mining done,
Unrestrained fossils burned,
Polluted air killed many people as a strong
reaction.

Still intelligent beings moved on with no
thinking,
No break on selfishness,
No care for Nature's world,
Could not even realize that air to breathe is
sinking."

Standing there with eyes wide open,
Impatiently started reading line-by-line, no
blinking.

The second sheet contained,
At the center, a drawing of an oval shop.
A big sign was put in front
Written in capital letters,
"BREATHING IS NOT FREE!"
As pure air sharply drops.
The second sheet contained,
At the center, a drawing of an oval shop.

Reading this line,
On the sign with a loud cry, I woke up.
Realized the truth in the dream,
Asked myself,
Will it really happen? While sipping tea from
my favorite cup.
Reading this line,
On the sign with a loud cry, I woke up.

'Blue Sky' - A Treasure of Beauty

Oh, Blue Sky!
Where do you start and where do you end? (I)

Nobody can see your complete form,
For scientists you remain a mystery,
For poets, a fascination,
Aestheticians cannot stop admiring your beauty
You are immeasurable in size and splendor.
Oh, Blue Sky!
Where do you start and where do you
end? (II)

Numerous stars, even bigger than the sun,
Find a little space inside you here and there,
How many Galaxies rest in your stomach,
Only you can say.
Oh, Blue Sky!
Where do you start and where do you end?
(III)

Clouds find their space in you to generate
Life in the form of rain,
A smile of comfort raises its head in the
hearts of withered plants,
Suffering animals and distressed humans
when raindrops touch the Earth,
The scorching heat of the summer retreats
back.
Oh, Blue Sky!
Where do you start and where do you end?
(IV)

Poet after poet placed you in their poems,
Never getting tired of describing your beauty,
Aestheticians pour out innumerable praises

for your beautiful looks through all days,
nights, and seasons,
Oh, Blue Sky!
Where did you get this gorgeous look? (V)

Whenever I see you in your colorful form,
Whenever I see you decorated with stars and
moon,
I wish to stand still and stare at you without
blinking,
Your soothing beauty, uninterruptedly
through my eyes
Travels straight to my heart,
And disperses all my worries
As a lamp pushes away vast darkness,
Happiness fills me with new energy all over
my body
As raindrops bring life to a dried garden.
Oh, Blue Sky!
Where did you get this gorgeous look?
Where do you start and where do you end?
(VI)

Armor

Nature loves humans like a mother loves her children

A love undeniable

No condition

No expectation

Busy arranging needs, always makes man's life lighten,

Food for stomach

Clothes for body

Shelter overhead

Double-checking the supply chain to ensure it continues unbroken.

Treasure is full, constantly replenished to be used by all

Each and for everyone
One and for all
The haves and have-nots
Fairness, equality, impartiality prevail as the
policy overall,
Power to eyes
Melody to ears
Aroma to nose
Delish to tongue, bliss to heart, peace to
mind, for big and small.

From where and how her children learned
such destructive greed
Decreasing Trees
Plummeting Fossils
Substandard Air
We got as a result of our back-stabbing
Nature at an uncontrolled speed,
How so cruel
How treacherous
Man can be
How imprudent to hope for Jasmine flowers
from cactus seeds?

Crossing all boundaries, Mother Nature's
patience is put to test
For how long
In what ways
Dam of patience
Can withstand continuous hits of wrong
deeds on its walls at its best,
Hurricane, Cyclone
Flood and Drought
Hinting frequently
The ultimate bang that could erase the human
race along with his nest.

Action is the only way out from here nothing
else can save,
Apply wisdom
Conscious minds
Perform together
Respect Nature, bowing the head,
Create enormous action waves:
Actions for Soil
Air, Water, Fossils
Oceans and Forests
Small and big can act as Armor keeping you
away from the grave.

'HE' versus 'SHE'

Unmindfully, I switched on the TV,
Sat in front to watch whatever came on
Without any choice.

From channel to channel I changed,
Without stopping my thumb from pressing
the button
On my slow-working TV remote control.

Then I paused, looking at a kitchen with two
windows
Big in size, one painted in olive green, and
the other, in red.

In front of the kitchen, a strong circular
wooden table,
A man and a woman sitting, facing each other
Both well-dressed and one with a mask.
Silence ruling, no talking
"What are you doing?"
Came out of my mouth.

I looked curiously at the info of the show
It was written
'HE' versus 'SHE'.
Silence broke. 'HE' asked 'SHE',
"Does it kill you? Do you believe?"
"I think a myth it is."

'SHE' stood up, went in the kitchen,
lit the stove, on the fire put a pan and
said, "I will prepare kheer for you."

Being perplexed 'HE' asked again,
'SHE' ignored, putting a tablespoon full of
homemade cow ghee
into the heating pan.

Irritated, 'HE' went near 'SHE' in front of the
window green,
Pulling down the mask, 'SHE' gave a smile.
Put organic cashews into the hot liquid ghee.
'HE' seemed lost, so was I,
"What is happening?" at the same time
asked 'HE' and I.

Without knowing what to do,
'HE' sat at the table, hands on his head
Kheer ready, told 'SHE' with a smile.

Stopped at the red window, poured the kheer
in two bowls,
and a few drops of chemical in one,
Putting on the table said 'SHE,' "This is with a
chemical and is for you."

"What is the chemical and why is it in mine?"
"Slow poison it is," humbly answered 'SHE'
"Are you crazy?" shouted 'HE'.
With more humbleness, 'SHE' asked,
"Does it kill you?" "Do you believe?"
"I think a myth it is."

Silence prevailed, 'HE' looked at 'SHE'.
"Please make it clear," begged 'HE'.
"If there is a link, I cannot see."
Putting a hand on HIS shoulder
Politely asked 'SHE,' "Saying no to slow
poison.
Then why yes to AIR POLLUTION?"

A Spectacular Gift of Nature

When the sun prepares to rest after a day of hard work,
When the sun starts reducing its strength of heat and light,
When the Earth begins welcoming temporary darkness,
The curtains of the day start dropping slowly,
And we enjoy the spectacular gift of Nature—the 'Evening Time.'

The western horizon prepares a velvety bed for the Sun to rest,

The western sky adorns itself in lively yellow,
orange, and red,
A miraculous, picturesque, and perfect
masterpiece of art,
Floats high up, clearing hearts and minds of
the day's stress,
Just like a fireplace that drives away the bitter
chill of a winter night.

Homecoming flying birds in magical shapes
look lovely,
Like the finest drawing with utmost
creativity, an artist has drawn,
The Moon from the eastern horizon peeps on
the Earth,
Waiting to shower its silvery cool gleam on
everything below,
Finding time appropriate, the Moon appears
With all its twinkling light-emitting heavenly
friends.

The sky fascinates us with its flowery ornate
lavish look,
A big umbrella designed with sparkling
diamonds, Stars and Moon,

Cool breeze penetrates deep into the body,
mind, and soul,
Taking in happiness, freshness, serenity and
relaxing power,
Delighted, I thank Nature for its incredible
gift—the 'Evening Time.'

Now or Never

Industries growing, nations fighting
Greeneries falling, fossils burning
Greenhouse gases meter riding
Take action radically oh! Man clever,
Nature shouting, "Time is Now or will come
Never."

Air polluting, soil infecting
Water miring, ecosystem fading
Fellow feeling in selfishness drowning
Take action radically oh! Man clever,
Nature shouting, "Time is Now or will come
Never."

Diseases spreading, humans dying
Bombs exploding, Nature crying
Potable water is declining
Take action radically oh! Man clever,
Nature shouting, "Time is Now or will come
Never."

Globe is warming; the climate, changing
Glaciers melting, sea level rising
Teasing mankind cyclones laughing
Take action radically oh! Man clever,
Nature shouting, "Time is Now or will come
Never."

The First Rain Drop

During my daughter's summer vacation,
Went to the village in mind
for a heat concession.
As hot as New Delhi, sweating all day,
Hot wind, no electricity, no sleep till
midnight,
Body demanding cold weather, mind asking
peace
but there was no relief in sight.

Every eye gazed up at the sky, expecting rain
to come,
Pacify Earth, plants and animals, else
living-dead they become.
"When will a gust of cold wind touch my body?"

"When can I escape the sizzling heat of the sun?"
"When can I sing the songs of relief?"
All these questions on my mind, with answers
none.

One fine morning, I started walking
completely absorbing the peace,
Capturing happy cool villagers, knowing the
glee was about to cease.
Wished the sun would not come
for the villagers' delight to last a bit more,
Reached under the banyan tree at one end of
my village,
Startled at the thunder's roar.

Looked up anxiously, perceiving chillness
along the spine,
Felt a drop on my nose, selfishly claimed the
'raindrop' as mine.

SA-RE-GA-MA

On a hot summer day at noon,
My mind was desperate for a heavenly boon.
Cool room and water were my only wish,
The burning sun and mulish sweat put me in
deep anguish.

No comfort from the natural and forced wind
I expected,
As with the fury of the sun and its own
swiftness, it was loaded.
But the trees in my garden turned things
around,
Amidst the heat, I discovered my joy had no
bounds.

Became active the leaves, dull they were a
moment ago,
As if the wind came with gifts that caused
their minds to blow.
Gloom faded, eyes glowed, leaves lost in
dance,
Like children with innocence without losing a
chance.

No care for boundaries and friction with
others,
Created great music when rustled with
brothers.
The wind earlier I showed no confidence on,
Reached me with a soothing sound, like to a
hungry man with a bag full of corn.

Nature's gentle voice reached my brain
through the ears and to the heart,
Delighted, I danced inside with the beautiful
Nature's art.
Heat had gone, happiness on, completely
absorbing the swish

Sadness gone, serotonin on, enjoying a life
lavish.

The coolness of streams, chirping of birds,
pitter-patter of rain,
Mother's lullaby, baby's cooing mixed with
the silence of the ocean.
All in a bundle came to me like the colors in a
hued rainbow,
Nature came near me, rustling with merriness
to bestow.

A Present to the Future

Over dinner on a hot summer evening
Climate-change was the topic hot,
Ever beautiful Mother Earth grieving
Her children drafting their own ending plot.
"Is this your present to me, oh! father?"
"Is this your gratitude towards your mother?"
asked a twin question, my dearest daughter.

Furnished everything you wanted each time
Still for Mother Nature respect naught,
Unbearable pain she gets from your crimes
No relief action and empathy nought
"Is this your present to me, oh! father?"
"Is this your gratitude towards your mother?"
asked a twin question, my dearest daughter.

Heatwave roaming around the street up in
arms
The same air once comforted man spreading
its charm
As if ready to burn everything down on its
way,
Ever increasing its fierce form on loud
display.
"Is this your present to me, oh! father?"
"Is this your gratitude towards your mother?"
asked a twin question, my dearest daughter.

Soil looks up for water, mouth wide open
Mother Nature is furious because of your
path chosen
Farmers dismayed, their tears unstoppable,
The same soil once filled all stomachs
gradually turns incapable.
"Is this your present to me, oh! father?"
"Is this your gratitude towards your mother?"
asked a twin question, my dearest daughter.

Cyclone has become a frequent event,
shattering everything it passes

In the aftermath, silence falls, time stops but,
people's ruination dances
Name is enough to produce a quake in one's
chest
All these happen because you put Mother
Nature's patience to the test.
"Is this your present to me, oh! father?"
"Is this your gratitude towards your mother?"
asked a twin question, my dearest daughter.

Disturbed in sleep and with agitated mind, I
thought
Conscious answers to the questions, I sought,
What kind of world are we building?
with Mother Nature no equation
What kind of presents are we saving to pass
down to the next generation?

A Cuckoo's Call

Far from a mango groove came a cuckoo's call.
Wind as a messenger, sweet voice it brought.
The voice captivated me as a lotus charmed by
the Sun,
Musicians of the world in front of it will feel
themselves small,
Far from a mango groove came a cuckoo's call.

What was it saying, what was it singing?
Not a single hint I got.
Still, yarn of multi-color actively my mind
spun.
In my heart, started to flourish beautiful
music tower tall,
Far from a mango groove came a cuckoo's call.

Mind relaxed, heart lightened,
As though the hunger had been satisfied after
days of plight.
Ears satisfied, soul satiated, stress undone,
In the sky of my mind, quite a big rainbow
sprawled.
Far from a mango groove came a cuckoo's call.

Like some drops of honey for a sweet craving
tongue,
Like some broken words from the mouth of a
tiny tot,
Like the beauty of a blooming rose encircled
by hurting thorns,
Like the nostalgic past happenings memory
recall,
Far from a mango groove came a cuckoo's call.

I Want you to Go away

I saw a giant, four times taller than me,
Legs like banyan trees, head a large globe, I
see.

Body of smoke, ash, and dust in different
degrees
Laughing louder than thunder, stood in front
of me.
Suddenly became million parts much smaller
than a flea,
Revolving around my head, buzzing like a
swarm of bees.

Irritated, I closed my ears and asked, "Who are thee?"
"Where are your endpoints, you appear as a sea."
"Damaging my eardrums your noise, your smoke killing we,"
"How can you, uninvited, move here so free?"

"Your deeds created me, your selfishness invited me,
I conquered your land as far as you can see.
I rule where I get conscience as an absentee,
Throw me out if you can, take actions of quality.
My name is Air Pollution, dying people, I like to count,
Every day I spread diseases, killing mass with no discount."

Blood boiled, eyes red, I shouted, "Go away,
Don't infest my pure air, leave this place right away."

Dream broke, I woke up with tachycardia perspiration,

Dried throat fast breathing mentally in deep
frustration.

Rang my scientist friend, described in vivid
the nightmare,
Wished some sympathy might come from
there.

"If we can kill our ego-centered self," said my
friend,
"Destructive path that we follow, if we can
mend,
Worshiping nature if we can make our trend,
Our hearts, if cry for quality of air to ascend,
Then only we have a chance to escape,"
concluded my friend.

Do not Test My Patience

Inside a theatre, people many,
From a projector focused on the screen,
a terrible scene.

The ground shook with a high-magnitude
quake.
Tsunami roared, volcanoes exploded
Clouds thundered, soil broke
From the core, Mother Earth came furious.

Shaking body anger at the peak
Eyes red, shooting fireballs on humans
Hands with damaging weapons
To punish mankind for deception.

Repeatedly screaming, "Do not Test my
Patience, oh! human."
People frightened, running for life
Desperate cries pleaded for mercy—
Mother's embrace, her kind protection
Repeated screaming, "Save us, Mother. Give
us life."

Mother Earth shouted,
"Fossils emptied, Air poisoned,
Soil tarnished, Water smudged,
Took me for granted
Even a bit of care shown not."

"Trees not spared, creatures ignored,
I, me, and myself only, second none,
This attitude brought you here
Get ready for penalty severe."
"Use scientific power
Muscles and money
Save yourselves from my wrath,
If you can."

"Face hotness, face cyclones
Frequent floods and droughts in queue."

Saying this, Mother Earth disappeared.

Pin-drop silence spread around.
Fearful faces, limbs paralyzed
Blank minds stood looking at each other.

The Pearl in my Garden

Walking bare feet on the grass carpet, my legs seized

Face frozen, eyes fixed on a dew drop

On a betel leaf, took a seat as my guest, I was pleased

Asked my mind, "A piece of divine pearl did somebody drop?"

A tiny ray from the sun it allowed to enter

Shined like a smiling baby I received from it, a treat visionary

My heart danced like a peacock in rain, filling bliss within

In the infinite sky of my mind, it rose as the
polestar glary.

Unknowingly, its soft form I touched as
gently as I could
Jumped to my ring finger, embraced as if
known forever
A shiver of thrill down my spine instantly ran
I wished to keep it with me together.

Inside the lifeless drop, I found something
striking and lively
It made my day, lightening my mood and
nourishing my soul
The odorless pearl, like tuberose smelled
widely
I became one with the dew drop, as the whole
of me it stole.

In the Flowing Tears

Drought-stricken land, debt-bound hand
In the north-eastern corner of his field, sat
the farmer
Looking down, then staring up, trying hard to
fight the defying tears
"When can I sow as the rain so late to come
this year?"
I saw Mother Nature in the flowing tears.

A two-year-old baby in the lap, under a
flyover seeking a nap
A part of her wet saree around the baby is a
little relief
Watching the miserable face of her child
trying hard to fight the defying tears

When the ire of the Sun calms down,
The mother thinks, "Why is it so hot again
this year."
I saw Mother Nature in the flowing tears.

"Heavy showers, severe flood came here to
suck my blood,
Shattered house and destroyed crops killing
me," said the villager.
Gazing at woeful children trying hard to fight
the defying tears
"Why more and more violent floods striking
now every year."
I saw Mother Nature in the flowing tears.

A tube in the nose, liquid food on a hospital
bed lying my friend
Never abused substances, offered healthy tips
to others, said a friend forever.
Little hope of surviving, doctor says, "It's
pollution,"
While saying this, the friend tried hard to
fight the defying tears.
I saw Mother Nature in the flowing tears.

'Re'- The needed Prefix

Discussing sustainability in a group
To form in the area a Green Warrior Troup.

What to do, what to say, and what to fix?
Somebody said, "'Re' is now the much-needed
prefix."

Rethink before you buy something
If you really need it to bring.
Separate wants and needs, do not mix,
'Re' is now the much-needed prefix.

Refuse poly bags and poly packs
non-decaying,
Poisoning Nature, strength displaying.

Think present, think future, and select your picks
'Re' is now the much-needed prefix.

Reduce waste, think smart,
Let unpackaged eco-friendly items fill your cart.
Build protective walls with layers of action bricks,
'Re' is now the much-needed prefix.

Reuse, Recycle, Repurpose—make this your life's battle cry,
Bring the Earth's former glow back home to the Sky,
If not, Nature's outrage will lead life on earth to complete nix.
'Re' is now the much-needed prefix.

Fidus Achates

Lotus on Earth and the sun, so far
Still acclaimed friends they are.
Lotus blooms when the sun it can see
Spreading divinity all around with beauty and
glee.

Root and soil share a bond, brotherly
Declare their trust in one another so utterly.
Root gives protection; soil supports the tree
In the face of danger, their unity is a thing
gutsy.

From its birth, River travels quite a long
Thinking only of meeting the ocean all along.

Ocean keeps its door open, one day its friend
will come
To become a part of its vast kingdom.

Flowers keep their nectar safe to feed the bees
At any condition, they do not allow their
amity to cease.
The duo together produce honey the sweetest
of all
They teach humans a life lesson even when
they are small.

With each other like born enemies, people
quarrel
Greed and jealousy take center stage in the
reign of the king immoral.
Small creations of Mother Nature
Live in harmony, work in favor.

How can man not sense them at all?
How can man avoid the call?
How can man not listen to Nature's Voice?
How can man ignore his only choice?

A Tribute

One said, clad in a brilliant green saree
Embroidered rainbow on its border
Black clouds as hair up to the waist
A glittering crown with stars embedded
On the forehead the sun sparkles
The moon dangled as the nose ring
Lightning decorates the eyes.

Another spoke, a stream comes out of the
smile
a beautiful garland of plaited flowers
From the neck down to the knees
Rivers around the waist as waist-girdle
Oceans readily protects the feet.

The third one spoke, the voice feels as calming
as the spring breeze
Sings songs of blessings in birds' twittering
Sitting gracefully on the Himalayas on a
throne of Sandalwood
Showering blessings on everybody with no
exclusion.

On my Facebook page commented three users
In response to my tribute to the beauty of
Mother Nature.

The Bow Strong and Wide

In the eastern sky, appeared a big bow
Ornated in seven colors layer upon layer,
strong and wide.
Vanished in no time, imprinting its beauty
to my heart's content.
Sweeping dirt away from my heart
strewing magic on me, off it went.

Taught a powerful lesson on unity
How to act as a robust community.
In all aspects different are the colors
United they appear white, diminishing
their individual characters.

Sent me a message loud and clear:
Matters not how long you live on earth
But it's *how* you live, that counts.
How high you flew, and how far you moved,
that counts.
"What have you done for your fellow beings?
What have you left for the generation to
come?"
That counts.

Drop by Drop Fills the Pitcher

Small words when weaved carefully
motivate even the most negative,
Small words, when arranged in fashion
in odd situations, set narrative.

A small well can quench thirst
of many a traveler passing by,
Lakes and rivers get filled by
little raindrops from the sky.

A small pen can shake the world.
A small pen can make the world.

A small story can melt a lot of hearts.
A small speech can build brave hearts.
Small actions have potential big.
A strong branch first starts as a twig.
Mastering tiny habits, one's character gets
richer.
Drop by drop fills the pitcher.

Save little drops of water at your home
whatever you can,
Save a bit of electricity whenever you can.
In your neighborhood plant a tree,
Help Mother Earth to be pollution-free.
Be part of fossil saving as much as you can,
Make 'Carbon offsetting' your mantra
in life, oh! clever man.
Don't doubt the effects of your tiny acts,
Pleasing flowers as you know, arise
from minute bracts.
Your single step has tremendous power
to boost the Nature,
Drop by drop fills the pitcher.

Beautiful Lotus

Grows in muddy water
Untouched and undeterred by the dirt
Symbolizes purity of heart and mind.
Represents long life, health, and hope
Regarded highly by Hindus and Buddhists
alike
Signifies manners, soft and kind.

Petals as soft as the palm of a newborn baby
Color pacifies the staring eyes,
Shriveling when the sun disappears
Happily, blossoms at sunrise.

One flower, uses many
Seeds as prayer beads, petals for worship
Roots and rhizomes as vegetables
Lotus pip as tea.
Some people make lotus silk
Some use its parts to heal
body and soul both alike
Mental harmony brings it to me
when I see.

In the nearby Forest

One fine morning as dawn came
to my courtyard to start a new day
Went walking to the deserted forest nearby.
Chose a narrow not much-trodden path
The green sea divided for me to walk
Forced my brain for a dopamine flow
and my mind to fly so high.
Spreading green carpet on the track
Swinging leaves welcomed me
Delicious greens into the body entered
through my hungry eyes.
Flowers gifted me pearls of dew
Talked with me in bird's voice soft and sweet
Slow cold wind touched my head
as if Mother Nature in disguise.

Closed my eyes artlessly face upward
Arms extended wide open
To absorb every bit of peace into the cells
deepest.
Felt like a chilled shower on a scorching day
Heavy head turned light, loaded heart empty
Gave my tired body shelter, the forest,
in his heart biggest.
Sitting on the top of an uneven rock
Staring at the greenery all over
Wanted to sleep on the lap of Mother Nature.
No need to look at the watch
No interest in going back
Wanted to swing in the arms of Mother
Nature.

Don't Play Victim

You are not the victim of cyclones.
You are not the victim of floods.
You are not the victim of water scarcity.
You are not the victim of homelessness
because the sea crosses its border.
You are not the victim of pollution-borne
diseases.
You are not the victim of Nature's rage.

Your bad situation was created by you.
You have imbalanced Nature's peace.
Wasted resources as if no tomorrow
'Don't care attitude' towards Nature's
warning

You have burnt fossil fuels with no control
Weaved a blanket of greenhouse gases over
your head
You, yourself, both oppressor and victim on
the stage.

Don't play victim, take action.
Only actions guarantee your protection.
Don't blame Nature, go closer.
Don't sit idle, worship the Mother.

From where it came

Mother Nature never kept her resources in
the treasury only for her,
Open-handedness prevails
greed exiled in the empire of her.
I cannot understand where this greed
came from, ruling the human mind and heart.

Tree gives fruit, flowers, and roots
leaves and trunk, even letting herself uproot.
No complaint only pleasure
Gratifying mankind's needs and greed.

Cloud pours whatever it has in the store
Emptying itself becomes happy to the core.

Never keeps anything for own use
To all on the earth granting life and peace.

Soil allows to draw water as much as we
require
Delivers food and minerals as we aspire.
Never asks anybody to stop even if drained to
nothing
Cheerfully builds man's demands and luxury.

Big-heartedness everywhere in the realm of
Mother Nature
Bounteousness teaches us in every step,
Mother Nature.
Can taste, feel, smell, see and touch
generosity all around
I cannot understand where this greed
came from, ruling the human mind and heart.

Between the Devil and the Deep Sea

Mother Nature sobbing, saying in a voice
trembling
"I am the mother, standing at the juncture
On one side the devil, the deep sea on the
other.
My heart bleeds when my own children do
not care for me
I cry secretly when the damage they cannot
foresee.
It hurts when those who receive everything
from me show no appreciation
Tears come down my eyes when I see

my children fight only for subjugation."

Mother Nature sobbing, saying in a voice
trembling
"I am the mother, standing at the juncture
On one side the devil, the deep sea on the
other.
My heart bleeds when my children cry in pain
Because of the ruin thrown upon them by the
cyclone chain.
I cry secretly when human settlements get
eroded
Severe floods unstoppable created by my
anger goaded.
It hurts me when death is the gift they receive
instead of my caring arms,
Tears fall down my eyes when my children
As a result of own actions bring themselves
awful harm.

Mother Nature sobbing, saying in a voice
trembling
"I am the mother, standing at the juncture
On one side the devil, the deep sea on the
other.

On one side ill-mannered humans, my
punishments on the other
At the juncture, I stood as a helpless mother."

All are Equal

In the eastern sky with energy inexhaustible
Every day to distribute comes the sun
Small and big, plants and animals—for
everyone free and accessible
With an open heart as per need, no
discrimination.

Rich or poor, healthy or ill, from one religion
or another
Comes touching every head on its way, no
biasness
Gives oxygen, maintains life, like for a child
does a mother
'Wind,' its name no desired fame, no
judgement in its heart's vastness.

Along the narrow path to the hill in my
lovely village
Indian jasmine flowers welcome all on the
way
Male, female, child, adult—granting nobody
any privilege
Sweet, rich, fruity sensual fragrance all
around, happily they spray.

River never asks your caste or class
Before allowing thirsty people to drink its
water so vivacious
River never asks where you come from
Distributes Life, no prejudice in heart and
mind so gracious.

Mother Nature knows no disproportion, all
are equal in her eyes
All resources she has for man's progress, she
supplies.
Many forms of disparity here and now, man
has created
Mankind made himself the prisoner of hatred.

Hope

Hope mankind will learn to behave
and respect Mother Nature,
To realize his deeds that cut his future.
Hope mankind will shed his egotistic eye
mask
and see what harm he has done already,
To understand the price he has to pay so
heavy.
Hope man, like today, will not stay passive
and take actions so massive
Hope for selfless people all around
busy creating an environment so conducive.

Hope Mother Earth becomes as beautiful as
before
and be cured again,
Hope Mother Earth on us happily
shower her blessings again.
Hope for water and air unpolluted
Hope for a peaceful life undaunted.
Hope for a world where brotherhood rules
No one sinks another's boat destroying venal
tools.

www.ingramcontent.com/pod-product-compliance
Lightning Source LLC
LaVergne TN
LVHW041223200726
843507LV00013B/2563